THE HARVARD BOYS CLUB

Hitler's assault on our freedoms from his grave

By

Jim Green

Dedicated To:

Christopher

ISBN-10: 1475210574

Copyright: TX-5-634-932

THE HARVARD BOYS CLUB

PROLOGUE

I had flown to Washington, D.C. from California—to influence the U.S. Supreme Court to hear a particular case.

In looking back, my chances were less than zero to the 10th power—this was the 4th or 5th time this case had been on the docket of the Court over the past 10 years—and they certainly had paid no mind to the violation of my Constitutional rights before—rights

barely visible in American jurisprudence—
rights held by an "employee" in America—

When we go to work in America, we cease to
be American citizens—and it wasn't that
many years ago that the U.S. Supreme Court
classified employee grievance cases under
"Master-Servant"—with "employee rights"
particularly relevant, today, given our
current unemployment crisis—and the
proliferation of workplace violence, as
documented in the just released movie
"Murder By Proxy".

One good thing did come from the trip—the
word "Club" used in the title—Carl Stern,
then Law Correspondent for NBC News, at
the time, counseled "You are dealing with a
club" regarding the judiciary in America—in

particular the federal judiciary, and I had filed a Complaint For Fraud against a club member--and even had all else been equal, I became persona non grata.

Indeed, at the Ninth Circuit, Anthony Kennedy—who had yet to be appointed to the U.S. Supreme Court, covered up this fraud by a federal judge in San Francisco—

But at no time did any of the judges reviewing this matter declare my Complaint to be "frivolous"—or definitely state that Schwarzer had not lied to deny to a U.S. citizen rights protected by the U.S. Constitution—thus leaving a cloud over the federal judiciary—and because, in fact, Schwarzer did lie [more on this shortly]—

Where it starts reading more like fiction, than fact, however—Schwarzer had been a Hitler Youth–he was born in Berlin, Germany on April 30, 1925, and had spent his formative years under the Third Reich. Membership in the Hitler Youth was mandatory in Germany, after 1936.

The reason Schwarzer's fraud is particularly egregious, aside from the fact that he lied to cover up criminal negligence on the part of the government defendants in our son's death in federal case C77-0307-WWS—

Once we accept the precedent that it is OK for a federal judge to lie to deny to a U.S. citizen, rights protected by the U.S. Constitution—where do we then draw the line saying is it not OK?

When this practice reaches our neighbor on our left, or our neighbor on our right—and on and on until we have no freedoms in America—

This fraud is not acceptable under *any* circumstances—not once—*not ever*!

It is a fraud that, absent surgical removal, has the potential to eat away at our Constitution like a cancer --The "equal protection" clause will not permit any other result—

And where perception gets distorted—judges "bending" the law to one's political persuasion is a common practice in American jurisprudence—the distinction is that fraud under this circumstance is "breaking" the law—it cannot under _any_ circumstances be made legal, and Schwarzer's fraud is absolutely unique in American jurisprudence.

In short, absent a reversal of Schwarzer's fraud—we may as well throw the Bill of Rights into an incinerator.

And the kicker is that Hitler may have undermined the freedoms of every citizen in America, from his grave—

Another factor regarding Schwarzer's fraud—the single thread that makes us a free people in America—is the certainty of a "legal remedy" when our Constitutional rights are violated—and absent a legal remedy, the Bill of Rights becomes a toothless tiger—not worth the paper they are written on—

The specific intent of Schwarzer, by lying, was to deny a legal remedy—Indeed, Schwarzer stated in the court record that the facts of this case "could not be trusted in the hands of a jury"—and he lied to make sure a jury would never hear the facts—our having our "day in court" be damned!

When the Supreme Court again denied certiorari in one of the filings—I included the following "cartoon" in my Petition For Rehearing [which is automatic in a denial]—

The Clerk of the U.S. Supreme Court called me at my office in California, and asked that

I withdraw the "cartoon", [a reprint from The NEW YORKER] from this Petition—which I refused, of course, based on the First Amendment—and where it remains to this day—

IN THE

Supreme Court of the United States

October Term, 1979

No. 79-1627

JAMES L. GREEN,

Petitioner,

VS.

"Excellent, excellent. A fine blend of truths, half-truths, and blatant falsehoods."

"Excellent, excellent..A fine blend of truths, half-truths, and blatant falsehoods."

CHAPTER ONE

THE UNDISPUTED FACTS:

"It is little wonder that truth is stranger than fiction, after all, fiction has to make sense."
Mark Twain

WHAT FOLLOWS is a personal odyssey when the Plaintiff in a civil rights action accidentally stumbled into the inner-workings of the dangerous police state agenda by elements of the extreme right [their agenda to this day]. The following is documented by court records and historical events:

In writing judicial decisions, most judges set aside a part of the document to outline those facts which are not in dispute. The following are the undisputed facts regarding a U.S. District Court case, currently on file in the Northern District Of California, in San Francisco: Docket No. C 77 0307 WWS-- NDC:

U.S. District Court Judge William W Schwarzer, to whom this case was assigned, is the only federal judge in America to have been born in Berlin, Germany (4/30/25) and to have spent his formative years under the adverse influence of the Third Reich.

Federal Judge Schwarzer falsely reported the facts in his Decision in the above case, with the _intent_ to vacate a U.S. citizen's protected legal rights, and to sidestep specific provisions of the U.S. Constitution, the first such fraud in American history. And this fraud is infinitely magnified since it regards the Bill of Rights, and gives a whole new meaning to the nonsensical propaganda by the ultra-right regarding "liberal activists judges". Enforcing the Bill of Rights is not a "liberal" idea.

Unlike other types of fraud, this fraud created a "legal imperative". Because of his position in our government, Federal Judge Schwarzer's fraud has the effect of throwing the Bill of Rights into an incinerator .

Once we accept that it is OK for a federal judge to use fraud as a tactic to vacate protected constitutional rights for U.S. citizens, where do we then draw a line saying it is not OK?

As any good attorney will confirm, this precedent has the potential to eat away at the Bill of Rights like a cancer.

It is the fact that this potential exists that makes it so dangerous.

Every federal judge in America is now free to use this same tactic to diminish our constitutional freedoms, with impunity.

The minute Federal Judge Schwarzer committed this fraud to paper, he destroyed the Bill of Rights in America. This fraud is not permissible..not once, <u>not ever.</u>

By lying, Schwarzer was also covering up criminal negligence on the part of the government defendants in this action, in the death of our six year old son.

In a letter from Simon Wiesenthal, in Vienna, Austria, he has argued for mitigation (1), and cited that Hitler Youth were not to be prosecuted under the terms of the Nuremberg Trials (1945-46). On the side of mitigation, it could be argued that Schwarzer is the innocent victim of an indoctrination with Hitler's ideas as a Hitler Youth (Schwarzer was 14 when he and his family moved from Germany in 1938; membership in the Hitler Youth was compulsory for all youth over age 10, after 1936 [Schwarzer was 11 at the time]—and an oath pledging allegiance to Hitler was mandatory).

On the other hand, why on Earth would anyone with this background be appointed to the federal bench?

(1) In his two-page letter, Mr. Wiesenthal speculated that Judge Schwarzer was probably Jewish, or of Jewish heritage [Schwarzer lists no religious preference in his bio--but if he was a German Jew, it would infinitely magnify his responsibility not to deny my rights of citizenship in America], and he went on to say that it was against Germany morality for non-Jewish Germans to leave Germany at that time

(1938). Frankly, it never occurred to me that Schwarzer should be prosecuted as a war criminal, but rather that his fraud should be exposed, and reversed, because of the danger it poses to our Bill of Rights. (Albeit, an effort to prosecute Schwarzer as a war criminal, even if unsuccessful, would certainly bring his fraud to light and result in a reversal).

Perhaps, because of his indoctrination in a government where civil liberties were non-existent, [and persons were stripped of their citizenship—identical in result, to the facts, here]--Schwarzer saw his fraud as little different than cheating on a golf score; but the reality regarding the above entitled action is that Hitler, by some insidious grip on history, has been able to contaminate the U.S. Constitution with his fascist ideas, from his grave....specifically the demise of individual civil liberties.

If my rights under the U.S. Constitution are not worth the paper they are written on— neither are _yours_--

Further, there are other inexplicable actions on the part of U.S. Government officials, at the highest levels of our government, in Schwarzer's ascendancy to the federal bench.

In the wake of the Watergate Scandal, Schwarzer was named to be the senior legal counsel to the PRESIDENT'S COMMISSION TO INVESTIGATE CIA ACTIVITIES IN THE UNITED STATES (The Rockefeller Commission). This appointment was made by then President, Jerry Ford, and at the behest of CIA Director George H.W. Bush.

As senior legal counsel to this commission, Schwarzer was in a position to control information on items the Commission set down for review and, the Commission did, in fact, decide to again review the Kennedy Assassination. This commission was set in motion to quell a public clamor for an investigation into CIA abuses by the Nixon Administration.

During the Watergate hearings, the public learned that Nixon had used the CIA to spy on American citizens and to use this information to his own political ends. To assuage the public outrage, Ford set up the commission, and placed it under the name of his then Vice-President Rockefeller (who was held in high esteem by the public). Ford and Bush then set up the commission so as to defeat its intended purpose and keep the public in the dark by naming Schwarzer [and those of like-mind] as the gatekeeper.

Also, it should be of more than passing interest that the reforms which did result by Congress passing the Foreign Intelligence Sureveillance Act (FISA) in 1978, as a direct result of the Rockefeller Commission, and limited as they were, to prevent unlawful intrusion into the private lives of American citizens—and which have all but been erased, post 9-11, by the very same right-wing clique which caused the abuses in the first place!

And evident by Bush's admission in December 2005, that he conducted illegal wiretaps on Americans [without a warrant], in direct violation of FISA!

In August 1976, and as an obvious payoff for his work on the commission, Ford named Schwarzer to be a U.S. District Court Judge in spite of the fact that he was not a U.S. citizen by birth (and in deference to the many highly qualified judicial candidates who were born in America) and in spite of the fact that Schwarzer had no prior judicial experience whatsoever! Six months later, the above case was assigned to Schwarzer.

In 1990, then President Bush, elevated Schwarzer to the coveted Directorship of the Federal Judicial Center in Washington, D.C.

In March, 1995, this organization published the document "Proposed Long Range Plan for the Federal Courts". A frightening prospect, given that Schwarzer sees nothing wrong with using fraud to vacate U.S. Citizen's protected constitutional freedoms.

Indeed, the real reason behind the desperate struggle to re-capture the White House by tarnishing Clinton and now Obama, is to pack the federal judiciary with right-wing ideologues, under Bush II, Pickering and Miguel Estrada, to carry out the "Plan"!

The proof of this was never more evident than when Bush made a plea, just before the 2002 election, for immediate confirmation of the right-wing ideologues he wished to appoint to the Federal Bench, and before the

Senate for confirmation. (Post election, Bush appointed Pickering to be a Federal Appellate Judge, via a "recess appointment", in spite of his earlier rejection by the Senate for "glaring racial insensitivity" and being anti-civil rights).

It is obvious by their vote in this election, most Americans simply do not see that controlling the Federal Bench is the _key_ to turning America into a Police State, and the demise of our freedoms in America!

And With "Citizens United" as Exhibit One—when scurrilous ultra-right appointments to the Court sold America down the river—to the highest bidder! And the integrity of the federal courts hit a new low when a federal judge in Montana sent a racially charged email in 3/12, to demean President Obama--

Thus we must not see Schwarzer's fraud, and federal judges of like mind, as an insignificant footnote, but rather of compelling public importance to Americans!

Upon his retirement, Schwarzer was given glowing praise for his work on the federal bench from his personal friend Chief Justice of the U.S. Supreme Court William Rehnquist (even though Rehnquist knew of his fraud).

The federal judiciary is that thin black line that stands between our freedoms in America and a tyrannical dictatorship. The historical role of the federal courts is to be the "guardian" of our constitutional rights.

Given the crucial role of the Federal Courts to our continued freedom in America, on April 18, 1984, I filed a Complaint For Fraud against Federal Judge Schwarzer, at the U.S. District Court in San Francisco. Five days after this case was filed, on April 23, 1984, Federal Judge Vukasin, to whom the case was assigned, entered an Order of Recusal, stepping aside from hearing the case.

For the next several months the case floated unassigned. I could not approach the bench with a motion; there was no judge to approach.

Most importantly, however, Judge Vukasin's Order of Recusal was confirmation that Schwarzer had, in fact, used fraud to deprive a U.S. citizen of his civil rights. The federal judiciary is notorious for dismissing cases as "frivolous" at the drop of a hat, and on the slimmest of evidence, if they have any basis whatsoever to do so. And particularly where the judiciary, itself, is being questioned.

The mere absence of an immediate dismissal of the Complaint as "frivolous" provides substantive proof that the fraud complaint against Judge Schwarzer is meritorious.

Federal Judge Schwarzer used fraud as a tactic to vacate a U.S. citizen's protected Constitutional rights—and to deny the rights of citizenship to a U.S. citizen--this is an undisputed fact.

CHAPTER TWO

MORE FACTS....

"It is dangerous to be right, when the government is wrong." Voltaire

Suddenly, on July 6, 1984, a case which it appeared might float unassigned forever-- Had to be disposed of immediately!

The Clerk of the U.S. District Court in San Francisco, called me at work to advise that the hearing had been scheduled for 10AM on the morning of July 12, 1984, allowing for less than a week to prepare.

The request for even a few days continuance to adjust around my work schedule, was expressly denied. The Clerk advised that James Browning, then Chief Judge of the Ninth Circuit U.S. Court of Appeals had named a Senior Federal Judge from Portland, Oregon to hear the case, and that he would fly down on the morning of the 12th of July.

San Francisco was a beehive of activity on the morning of July 12, 1984, with 20,000 extra reporters in town, and the frantic efforts to put the final touches on the city for the opening of the Democratic National Convention, on July 16, 1984.

An FBI agent stood next to the U.S. Attorney, who flipped open his coat during the hearing to let me know he was wearing a gun and that he was ready to blow me to Kingdom Come if I made a false move....all I was armed with was words--

On July 16, 1984, the same day the Democratic National Convention opened, Senior Federal Judge Belloni, from Portland, rendered his Decision. Judge Belloni dismissed the case on the premise that Schwarzer could not be sued for "money damages".

Inexplicably, however, Belloni did not go on to make a finding that the Complaint For Fraud that had been brought against Schwarzer was without merit. Such a ruling was essential to answer the Complaint and also to remove the stain raised by this Complaint. It was a glaring omission and added even further proof that the charge of fraud (a criminal offense) brought against Schwarzer is true; and that Schwarzer had, in fact, lied to vacate a U.S. citizen's protected Constitutional rights.

Another interesting aside, at one point during the many months when the case was floating unassigned, I went to the U.S. Attorney's Office with a document of some kind (I don't recall what now) .

The receptionist apparently thought I was an attorney, and led me through the honeycomb of offices to the U.S. Attorney's Office. There was a large gathering of attorneys in his office, and they were discussing this case. The U.S. Attorney became flushed with anger at the receptionist, and he took both of us by the arm, one of us on each side, like a Kindergarten teacher scolding students, and led us back to the reception desk. At that point he held his hand up over my head and said to the receptionist in an angered tone "Don't ever let this person in here again"! As the U.S. Attorney knew well, he should have been prosecuting rather than defending Schwarzer.

Ironically, and perhaps known to the FBI and to the federal judiciary, my cousin, Fred Brown, was the Democratic National Committeeman for the State of Kansas and was at the convention in San Francisco.

With a petition signed by 200 Delegates to the convention, I could have addressed the convention, and exposed this egregious fraud, and tightly held secret by the federal judiciary, to the rest of the nation (unfortunately, I became aware of this procedure only much later). Indeed, perhaps it was in anticipation of this scenario that caused someone in the judiciary to panic and to force the dismissal of this action on an urgent schedule.

Just 10 days earlier, it appeared they were satisfied to let this case float unassigned forever.

On the night of Wednesday, July 18, 1984, my cousin was finally able to get extra tickets so that I could attend the convention. For the great majority who have been spared this experience, it is total chaos. It was a great evening to attend, however, and it was the evening Mondale accepted the nomination and made history by naming Geraldine Ferraro as the first female candidate for Vice- President.

The tickets for admission on to the convention floor were embedded with a holograph and perforated along the bottom for a quick detach. The ticket was to be worn around the neck at all times. The tab at the bottom contained certain basic personal information, including the party who arranged for admission; and the ticket was designed so that the tab at the bottom could be easily removed by convention authorities and the information quickly telegraphed to police authorities in the event of any hostile or aggressive behavior.

Also, the color of the ticket one received provided a quick reference to convention authorities as to how far one was permitted to advance on the convention floor. For instance, I was given a delegate's ticket, which placed my point of advancement pretty far back from the podium (it appears that politicians are not all that trusting of the delegates).

My cousin, on the other hand, had a ticket which permitted him to actually walk on to the podium, had he had reason to be there. All of us civil types, of course, welcomed, rather than resented, this convention structure given the history of violence in America.

Having had a couple of days to plan and having good reason to be cynical about the system and a corrupt judiciary, I took certain steps to expose this fraud before going to the convention, which gave no little concern that I could be arrested.

Earlier in the day, on July 18, 1984, I took my cousin and his wife out to lunch in Sausalito. Throughout the lunch I had planned to lay out the case I had filed in federal court and explain the danger to the Bill of Rights by leaving Judge Schwarzer's fraud on the books. But, as this very pleasant lunch went on, I just couldn't get out the words "I sued a federal judge for fraud"; and an inner voice told me that if I did, I would damn sure not be attending the Convention that evening.

In preparation for attending the convention, I had prepared 500, one- page leaflets entitled "IS THE AMERICAN PRESS DEAF, DUMB AND BLIND?" It has been my contention for many years, and I am even more convinced, given the Monica nonsense, that the American press has lost its way.

The constitutional basis for a "free" press is to warn the American people when their constitutional freedoms are in jeopardy; and few cases could better underscore the need for this constitutional protection of our freedoms.

When the press drifts from their constitutional mandate, however, then the American people have lost the benefit of having a "free" press and could well result in losing our freedoms.

Unfortunately, the press today is about making money, and "gottcha" nonsense is used to replace protecting our constitutional freedoms--and the indifference to the issues raised in this case, alone, is consummate proof.

The temporary tent set up outside of the Moscone Convention Center, where guests to the Democratic National Convention received their tickets, was filled with security types, as my cousin stood next to me to assist in getting a ticket. This was no place to have been carrying a ream of leaflets calling the American press deaf, dumb and blind; and I left the box for same in the trunk of my car.

The chaos on the convention floor actually assisted in my plan to deliver a copy of my leaflet to every press booth in the convention hall, no easy task under any circumstances, and in a situation where it seemed there were more press booths than newspapers in America.

About an hour into the festivities, I excused myself to get a Coke and hot dog. Given the long lines, this assured my cover for at least an hour. Instead of getting refreshments, however, I walked to my car, about two blocks away, and retrieved the leaflets from the trunk. I had thought ahead, a bit, and had limited the documentation to one page, thus avoiding staples which might have set off the metal detectors when I returned to the convention hall.

There was a multi-stage security checking system at the entrance to the hall, which, given the history of violence against our political leaders in America, is an understood and expected requirement at these type of events.

I slid the typing paper box on to the conveyor belt so that it could be x-rayed. I tried to look like what I was doing was "normal" (albeit, it was anything but normal..the protestors were a safe two blocks away..out of shouting range of the festivities); and I was not sure what would happen. I worried how I would explain to my cousin, if I had been arrested. I considered that they might not allow me to bring the box into the convention center at all, or worse prevent me from re-entering the convention.

My nerves were shot. After several nervous moments as the box passed through the x-ray machine, and the other x-ray equipment revealed I had no weapons on my person, they handed the box back to me.

I am convinced, in retrospect, that our personal appearance goes a long way in these security checking profiles (students frequently remark that I have a resemblance to Leslie Nielsen and like him or not, I just didn't fit the stereotype of a mad bomber, etc.).

With box and contents in tow, I took the elevator and headed to the upper levels of the convention center, looking for press booths. The search was short-lived, and in each case I tried to leave a copy of my document in the "IN BOX" in each press booth, if I could find one.

In some cases I would hand the paper directly to a reporter, such as the New York Times, etc. The paper documented that Judge Schwarzer had used fraud to vacate a U.S. citizen's protected constitutional rights and that federal judges at the highest levels of the Ninth Circuit U.S. Court of Appeals, for what ever their reasons, were trying to cover up this fraud, the Bill of Rights be damned!

The paper included the docket number of the case and my home telephone number so that follow-up to the charges could be readily investigated.

From the top level of the convention hall I worked my way down, a floor at a time. It seemed like a million miles of cable covered the floor of the convention hall so that not even one word of this historic event would be missed. But what could be more important to a free country than the fact that Hitler's ideas (whether by accident or design) had been used to contaminate the U.S. Constitution? Was anyone listening--

Back on the convention floor, I handed a copy to Sam Donaldson. I had the sense of having invaded his "royal presence", and as the "year of Monica" has shown us, Sam is out for Sam. If it smells like money for himself and ABC, Sam is interested; but protecting the individual civil liberties of ordinary citizens, forget it!

Seeking the "status quo", or "don't rock the boat", seems by far to be the standard followed by our "free" press, apparently no matter how egregious the crime against our individual freedoms.

Our Bill of Rights are hedged in such a manner so as to guarantee the preservation of all of our freedoms.
We have free speech [First Amendment] to complain if a court denies our right to a jury trial [Seventh Amendment] and a free press

[First Amendment] to expose this judicial corruption, etc.

But if apathy or money or whatever renders this process inoperable, then woe be to us, for we will not be free much longer; and in the aftermath of the events of 9-11-01, it should be clear that our civil liberties are tenuous, indeed.

Shortly after the dismissal of the Complaint For Fraud, I appealed to the Ninth Circuit U.S. Court of Appeals, and the case was assigned to Anthony Kennedy. Judge Kennedy quickly signed an Order closing the case against Schwarzer "with prejudice" to prevent a jury from hearing the facts—outlined, herein....

Appealing this matter to the U.S. Supreme Court in a fruitless effort to seek a judicial remedy was not new, and five times between the late '70s to mid-80s this case was on the docket of the U.S. Supreme Court (each a monumental task in itself).

At the behest of the high court, and unlike earlier filings they demanded that I print the Complaint For Fraud petition (at no small cost, as compared to sending a typed copy).

In my Petition for Rehearing (which is automatic), after the Court denied certiorari [in one of the filings], I incorporated the "cartoon" –a reprint from The New Yorker magazine (see above).

As a brief follow-up, in 1988, when Anthony Kennedy was named to the U.S. Supreme Court, by then President Reagan, I complained as loudly as I could to the powers that be in the senate confirmation hearings, regarding his unwillingness to remand this matter for a jury trial (i.e., that he was covering up this fraud, a criminal offense).

My complaints fell on deaf ears. Also, it seems of more than a passing interest that Kennedy served on the Board of Directors at the Federal Judicial Center (as noted above, senior Bush named Schwarzer to be the Director of the Federal Judicial Center, in 1990).

As we all know, now, it was Justice Kennedy who spearheaded the action to shut down the vote counting in Florida (that Saturday was Kennedy's "duty" day at the Court), thus guaranteeing the High Court's appointment of George W. to the Presidency in the 2000 presidential election--our democratic form of electing presidents be damned!

To illustrate the significance of Kennedy's appointment, the following is a very possible scenario, had Kennedy _NOT_ been confirmed by the Senate for covering up Schwarzer's fraud in the above matter:

The votes in Florida are counted and as everyone knows--Al Gore is elected President. The debt is paid down to the benefit of all Americans, and America is spared the same disastrous policies used during the Reagan Administration, which almost destroyed our country. President Gore actually listened to our counter-terrorist office, and Mossad (Israel's CIA) with the same warning, on August 6, 2001, of an imminent airline attack--and 9-11 was foiled--it never happened.

Also, the War on Iraq never happened, nor the War on Afghanistan, nor the War on Terror—nor the trillions in debt piled on the American people by these un-funded wars!

The house of cards known as the Enron Corporation, collapsed from the efficacy of its own pyramid scheme--on schedule. Several of the now Cabinet members in the Bush Administration, including Dick Cheney, are indicted as co-conspirators in this scheme.

In short, America was not set on its current perilous course, and the collapse of our economy in 2008, and a $14 trillion deficit [including mop up costs]--because Kennedy was denied appointment to the U.S. Supreme Court....

The name "The Harvard Boys Club", incidentally, was coined from the fact that Anthony Kennedy, William Schwarzer, and Douglas Hickling (the government official who was criminally negligent in our son's death--and Defendant in the above cited action) were all graduates of Harvard Law School, and all fellow members of the

Olympic Club, a private men's club in San Francisco.

Indeed, those with a long memory will remember the public uproar re Kennedy's membership at the Olympic Club (because of its racist policies and anti-semantic practices—and certain evidence that Schwarzer is not Jewish, or has rejected Judaism), and Kennedy had to resign and publicly denounce his membership in the Olympic Club.

Also, it needs to be noted that the title, here, is *not* a resentment, or contempt for Harvard, or whatever—I have enormous respect for Harvard and they have produced some outstanding Americans, such as

President and Michelle Obama—this is about three of their bad apples--

A couple of anecdotal asides, at one point two "men in black" came into my office (I owned a real estate office in Hayward, California, at the time), ostensibly to get a paper notarized. These were large, imposing guys who were literally dressed in black suits--they just didn't look like my usual clients.

While one distracted me with a notary request, the other walked around my office, opening closets and walking into the back room. Startled by this intrusive conduct, I stood up and said "What the Hell do you think you're doing?"

Obviously, my better judgment should have deferred to their size, and it was clear that they felt they were above answering this question. The other then reached in his pocket and pulled out a crumpled $5 dollar bill and dropped it on my desk (the usual, although not necessarily the cost for notarizing a document--but an inner voice told me this was no time to haggle over price).

My real estate office was really a front for carrying on my crusade against Schwarzer (although I had a small real estate business), and I kept the copy machine busy cranking out documents about ignoring the danger in Schwarzer's fraud.

As if being let in on a gag, although the atmosphere was very tense, I handed each a copy of "Is The American Press Deaf, Dumb and Blind"--as I looked towards the door, and indicated (very politely, of course) that they should leave and that I was not fooled by their unlawful intrusion. To this day I do not know if they were FBI, CIA, the Mafia-- but about one thing I am absolutely certain, they were not there to get a paper notarized.

At one point, during an appeal to the U.S. Supreme Court, I flew to Washington D.C. I had been corresponding with Carl Stern, then Law Correspondent For NBC News in DC, who covered the Court. My meeting with Mr. Stern at the NBC studios on Kansas Avenue, was a surprise to both us (to this day I do not know why in the Hell I thought at the time an ordinary citizen could influence the Court to hear a case).

Mr. Stern was very courteous and took me back to his office, which to my surprise, and as with all of the Correspondents, wasn't much larger than a closet. Most of their work is carried on from remote locations. I sat quietly as he made several follow-up calls to government agencies, on pending cases. He then looked at me with a wry smile and said "Damn bureaucrats" (Which, ironically, he became, and admirably represented, during the Clinton administration).

Mr. Stern gave me a ride back to Lafayette Circle so that I could catch the Metro back to my hotel. In our casual conversation, it seems that one of his twin sons had broken his arm and he was concerned with the outrageous medical bill he had been sent. He also counseled that I was dealing with a "Club", which contributed to the title. I would only add that Carl Stern is one of our most distinguished newscasters, and his article in The Responsive Community [type in Carl Stern via Google] is must reading on the subject of responsible journalism.

ADDENDUM TO CHAPTER TWO:

Me and the IRS

This book has been in progress for 30 years—and I have forgotten much--on purpose—but some anecdotal segments should be included—

Part of what was going on here is what I call "bureaucratic intractability" --When someone in a bureaucracy screws up— badly—and rather than admitting that the bureaucracy has made a mistake, the other bureaucrats circle the wagons in a sort of "We don't make mistakes, we are perfect, or above the law", or whatever—[and the etiology is almost always "low self-esteem"]--

It is a toss-up whether a psychiatrist or a priest is needed to treat this malady.

And, we are seeing this more and more with the discovery of DNA, where a person is released from death row because of DNA evidence—but are there because of a zealous prosecutor, etc., --who hides evidence to cover-up rather than admit that they— sometimes knowingly--charged the wrong person—and apparently would allow an innocent person die rather than have to admit--That they made a "mistake"!

In any event, at some point in the 1980's—I don't recall now which year—I calculated what my back pay would have been had Schwarzer complied with the legal remedy mandated by the U.S. Constitution—and recorded it as a loss on my income tax.

At the bottom of the 1040 I then wrote "No Income" [and given my Spartan existence— this wasn't far from the truth even absent this deduction].

For five years I didn't hear anything from the IRS, and I was beginning to think that they agreed with this deduction—I was wrong—

Also, in the meantime, I had moved to Texas from California—and most of my experience with the IRS was in Texas—and in particular with the massive IRS office in Austin, and branch offices from there.

As some may recall, in February 2010, an irate tax rebel flew his small plane into the IRS facility in Austin, causing extensive damage—it was initially thought to be another terrorist attack—

But a truism, the IRS does not take kindly to tax rebels—persons who are simply opposed to paying taxes--and in their minds they are Public Enemy Number One!

Much of my experience with agents in South Texas was their sorting out if I was a "tax rebel" or a "misguided idealist"—given their aggression at the beginning-- I was definitely classified as a "tax rebel"—and they threw a bunch of numbers at the wall and declared that I owed the IRS close to $18,000—which given what I would have paid with the usual deductions—was patently absurd!

I did stop taking the deduction after that, however—and I was hardly a "tax rebel"— for most of my employment [a cumulative 20 years as a probation office and chief probation officer] my income was from taxes.

Nevertheless, the IRS filed a tax lien for $17,000 plus, at my local court house, and then notified all of the three major credit reporting bureaus of this "debt" due to the IRS—it is the top item on the credit report-- and which they were more than happy to make any potential lender aware of—

This, of course, has a very chilling effect for any potential mortgage holder—or lender, in extending credit—the IRS is adamant in getting their money ahead of any lender in recovery from a default—as every lender knows—

In 1992, I reached an agreement with the IRS on taxes due in what they call "An Offer In Compromise" –I paid them $ 1,500—and my back taxes were then--"Paid In Full"—

The IRS also filed a "Release of Lien" which is on file at the court house—and I sent a certified copy of the release to all three credit reporting bureaus—end of story---right?

Wrong!

In spite of certified evidence that the lien had been paid--For years—all three of the agencies continued to include the lien as part of my credit report!

And getting it cleared up with the credit bureaus was akin to human Super Glue, and it would soon re-appear with their inbreeding—and to this day it is still on the credit report of one agency!

At one point I filed for a court hearing on the legitimacy of my deduction with the IRS, and a traveling circuit tax judge [the equivalent of a district court judge—but limited to tax matters] from DC heard my case—in San Antonio.

And oddly, or at least it seemed odd to me at the time, the tax judge asked me in detail about Christopher's diagnosis, i.e., Pulmonary Fibrosis—but in the end she ruled with the system—she wasn't about to blow the cover on Schwarzer's fraud, which denied my rights under the U.S. Constitution!

Almost without exception, the IRS agents that I dealt with in Corpus Christi, Austin and San Antonio, both "got it" and were sympathetic—and I got the sense that they would have allowed the deduction if they had the power to do so—

And at the court hearing a large number of agents, many I had never seen before, showed up for this specific hearing—some I suspect to see "Who is this crazy guy"—

Some of the best insight into this matter, however, was from an IRS agent in San Antonio—who looked at me quizzically [and mildly lecturing] said "You were trying to be creative in a bureaucracy"? --regarding the memo I wrote in Alameda County—which set all of this in motion—

CHAPTER THREE

THE UNDERLYING FACTS....

It is a curse, not a blessing to be creative in a police state - Albert Einstein

Given the oxygen-starved altitude in Denver, the only therapy the doctors could offer was to place Christopher on oxygen 24 hours a day. His doctors urged us to move to sea-level as soon as possible. I immediately went to California, hopefully to find employment in my chosen profession as a probation officer.

The Doctors in Colorado recommended San Francisco, San Diego, Boston or New

Orleans, given the dual criteria that these cities had excellent medical facilities as well as being at sea-level. I readily passed the Civil Service Exam for Probation Officers in Alameda County, California (a suburb of San Francisco), and from the date Christopher was first diagnosed, until we were living in California, was less than six months.

We must have looked like a scene out of the Grapes Of Wrath, as we trekked along at dusk on the high plateau which separates the Rocky Mountain and Sierra Nevada mountain ranges; with a U-Haul truck pulling our family car, and my wife in the second car, pulling our boat. A constant source of oxygen for Christopher was a concern in this sparsely populated region in the event of car trouble or an unexpected delay.

It was an enormous relief when we finally reached the more oxygen-rich sea-level in California, and we shouted out each thousand foot marker "4,000, 3,000, 2000, 1000" as we descended down the mountain towards Sacramento.

The officials in Alameda County were fully aware that our move to California was on an emergency basis to seek medical treatment for Christopher. Alameda County, incidentally, is one of the largest counties in the U.S., with a population larger than some of our states.

A doctor at the University of San Francisco Medical School felt that our only real solution was a lung transplant, which at that time was more akin to science fiction, than medical reality, and had never been tried.

The real blessing, however, is that at sea-level, Christopher, could get around without the constant need for oxygen, and for the first couple of years we moved back to an almost normal family existence, save for Christopher's periodic need for hospitalization. At work, I became a "tenured" employee and was rated by my supervisor as "exceeding the requirements" for my work.

Also, I was elected to be on the board of directors with the Trans-Bay Probation

Officers Association; and given my creative bent, I designed a statistical program for combining the pre-sentence report with a statistical gathering apparatus, so that we in Corrections could implement programs which would actually prevent future crime. Entitled B.R.I.D.G.E. (and not unmindful of the Golden Gate) the full name was "Basic Research In Design, Growth and Education".

I did not see it at the time, but any program which might actually solve our crime problem in America is perceived as a threat to the great majority in Corrections (there are a few exceptions, very few); and thus in hindsight it is a sad fact but the last person the American people should call upon to help solve our insidious crime problem is our "experts", because they are not interested in preventing crime! Indeed, the more crime the better, regardless of their statements to the contrary, because in their twisted perception this might cost them their "job", and irrespective of how many innocent persons are killed by their indifference!

To illustrate the point, and not to get too far ahead of myself, when Texas was floating bonds in the early 90's in preparation for the largest prison building spree in American history, a chief probation officer admonished his staff "Now you will want to vote for these bond issues because it will mean more jobs for us"!

When FBI statistics reported an increase in crime in Texas, last year, it was obvious that this massive prison building program was not the solution, but in this "small-minded" mind-set, actually trying to make America safer is not even on the table!

In spite of the successes during our first two years in California, both as regards Christopher and at work, there was a problem with "low morale" in the Alameda County Probation Department and the administration solicited and encouraged suggestions from staff, ostensibly to correct the problem. Given my mid-western upbringing, my response was the same as stopping to help a neighbor fix a flat tire. In retrospect, the administration's true agenda was to find a scapegoat to blame, and thus deflect the problem away from their poor management.

In response to their solicitation, I prepared a memorandum outlining four constructive suggestions which I felt would help to alleviated the problem of low morale among staff. I submitted the memorandum, and then left for a three week vacation and family reunion in Kansas.

When I returned, I was confronted by the office supervisor and told if I did not immediately withdraw the memorandum that I would be fired on the spot! I was given the lunch hour to think it over. The suggestions were singularly constructive, and included such innocuous suggestions as the creation of a "floating clerical position" to help alleviate the probation officer's paperwork (a major source of low morale). As I found out later, they found this suggestion to be particularly threatening to their authority. They preferred to see probation officers as children (even though a degree was an employment requirement). I had Christopher's welfare to consider and his hospitalization plan was critical to our medical options.

But withdrawing the memorandum, (not only devoid of rational human thought, but also in violation of the First Amendment) was not a solution ..I learned you cannot make peace with persons who are evil. I was transferred to a hostile supervisor, and denied transfer to another department. Over the next six months, they tried to create a paper case against my work, in complete deference to my earlier excellent evaluations.

It is difficult to fathom the depravity of the small-minded and the evil, but being the cowards that they were, and knowing full well that this was "blacklisting", they called my wife on Christmas Eve, to tell her I was fired, they didn't have the guts to tell me to my face!

The U. S. Supreme Court set down the "due process" law under the United States Constitution, for "tenured" employees under this exact circumstance [ARNETT v KENNEDY, 1974] . The High Court ruled that a tenured employee has a "property" interest in continued employment, and thus is entitled to "due process" under the 14th Amendment.

Specifically, this "due process" included: The right to a pre-termination copy of the written charges upon which the termination is based; compliance by the agency with their applicable "rules and regulations" ("due process" by definition); and the right to a "speedy" post-termination civil service hearing.

I immediately appealed for a civil service hearing. Their "rules and regulations" mandated that the hearing "must commence within 10 working days of the filing of an appeal, and to be concluded as quickly as possible".

In Fact: the start of the hearing was delayed for over three months (so they could prepare their "charges"--a major complaint was that my "handwriting is poor"); and the agency dragged the hearing on without resolution for almost *three years* (the longest in California history)!

Christopher passed away a year after the hearing started, two days after his sixth birthday. During that year my hair turned from dark brown to almost gray due to the agency's *intentional* delays (and the delays, singularly, were because they did not have a case for termination—there was *no* justification for this termination)! And other agencies would not hire me during a pending hearing because I may be reinstated--

No rational person could conclude that this was a "speedy" hearing, and Schwarzer lied when he ruled, by Summary Judgment, in Federal Civil Rights Case: C-77-0307-WWS, that the government officials "complied with their Rules and Regulations" (1).

When Schwarzer lied by stating that the applicable "due process" law had been "complied" with, he also rendered the U.S. Constitution feckless! This ruling is a blatant fraud, with far-reaching implications:

First, it vacated our right to a jury trial, where we could have a fair hearing on the facts [a Seventh Amendment right], and a subsequent legal remedy against the Defendants. Most significantly, however, this fraud was intended to negate our Constitutional rights as U.S. Citizens!

IF we don't have constitutional rights, neither does any other citizen in America (the "equal protection" clause allows for no other conclusion). The net effect of Schwarzer's fraud was to vacate our citizenship, as U.S. citizens--which is all the more remarkable given the fact that the was a tactic used by Hitler during the Third Reich!

Had Schwarzer told the truth when he made this ruling (that the Defendant's had "not complied"), he would have had no choice but to apply the remedy required by law under the Constitution.

(1) To state that the government officials violated their "rules and regulations" sounds pretty innocuous--but these were not mere

"rules and regulations"--in this instance, they were *legal rights protected by the U.S. Constitution* a fact, Schwarzer was fully aware of! Further, Schwarzer was fully aware that the violation of a citizen's constitutional rights, in this instance, held the potential for a direct and adverse impact on the healthcare of a small child, and thus, by their failure to comply the government officials were criminally negligence in Christopher's death!

To use a metaphor with the Trayvon/Zimmerman travesty—the government's violation of our constitutional rights was the 9mm—i.e., medical options which may have been available had been intentionally stolen away!

In short, given the circumstances of Christopher's illness, Schwarzer's lie—is a grotesque lie!

Criminal Negligence is defined in the law as a wanton disregard for how a reasonable and prudent person would act under like circumstances. Federal Judge Schwarzer's lie, as he intended, was also to cover up the Defendant's Criminal Negligence, in Christopher's death. If the Defendants had complied with the Bill of Rights, the "due process" set down by the high court, Christopher might still be alive.

In his book, "Freedom Inside The Organization", Dr. David Ewing penned, "Employee rights are like a black hole in space, so impacted by tradition that light can barely escape". In the years since Dr. Ewing made that observation, workplace violence has escalated into an almost daily occurrence because of our unwillingness to place our newest civil rights movement on the table so that we can discuss "problem solving" solutions.

Indeed, when I originally committed this to paper, Michael McDermott was on trial for murdering seven of his fellow co-workers, and incidents of workplace violence in the U.S. Postal Service have been too numerous to cite individually; just to name those which have become notorious, and in deference to the hundreds of incidents of workplace violence, per U.S. Department of Labor statistics, which go unreported by the media every year.

By our indifference to this new movement, the message to the American worker is quite clear: If you have a grievance, become violent, otherwise the media will pay no mind to your grievance. It is clearly the wrong message, and highly irresponsible on the part of the press to send this message. I am quite sure that if I were a violent person, I would be in prison in California, as a result of the events above, and I would be remiss in denying that I had violent thoughts.

To those who still do not see the larger picture. The violation of a citizen's constitutional rights is a *damage*, irrespective of any other injuries. But unlike other situations where persons are damaged, such as a result of medical malpractice, an auto accident, etc., if the courts will not provide a *remedy* when our constitutional rights are violated, then our Bill of Rights become worthless, a toothless tiger--of no value.

And it is on the strength of this single fact, *alone*, the absolute assurance that we have a *legal remedy* when our constitutional rights are violated, that allows Americans to claim that we are a free people, and it is this tiny thread, *alone*, that protects our 323 million Americans from a tyrannical dictatorship! We have nothing else.

I did not declare what my constitutional rights were in this case--the U.S. Supreme Court did.

ADDENDUM

As a response to the above, I put together certain proposed system changes we need to make--and have identified as Economic Inclusivism—it is outlined in detail at www.Inclusivism.org

It is difficult to pick an exact point at which the seeds for Economic Inclusivism started fermenting (albeit a name unique to this program was light-years away)..but it would probably be the Fall of 1969, only a few months before Christopher was born. We had moved from Kansas to Golden, Colorado, where I took employment with the Jefferson County Juvenile Court. Some have marked November 22, 1963, as the day "we lost our innocence"--and if this odyssey revealed anything to me, it is that our system is seriously broken--and that we are in dire need of systemic change.

When we moved to Golden, Colorado, we had never heard of Rocky Flats, a plutonium manufacturing plant run by Dow Chemical, some ten miles away. On May 11, 1969, only a few months earlier, the plutonium spontaneously ignited, and a fourth of the plant burned to the ground.

Indeed, the public statements by the AEC (Atomic Energy Commission), were very publicly soothing and held that no "significant" levels of plutonium were released into the atmosphere, but studies conducted by the government (not released to the public), revealed an unusually high number of deformed cattle started turning up--as well as accelerated cancer rates, and fibrosis of the lungs, in laboratory animal experiments.

We did not learn the devastating details of this fire until several years later when we were living in California. Quite by accident the subject came up, when a physicist friend started explaining what really happened at Rocky Flats. What we learned is that during the fire the plutonium formed into tiny crystals which not only saturated the ground downwind from the plant, but also became airborne, and that an unknown quantity of plutonium was lost.

We also learned that while the AEC was playing down the danger of the fire at Rocky Flats--at the same time they were quietly placing wind receptors around the Denver area to detect the levels of contamination.

Another factor were the periodic "Chinook Winds" which came racing down the canyon above Boulder on a direct path across this plant and into Denver, sometimes reaching 100 MPH--and thus making the control of these tiny plutonium crystals impossible.

The Rocky Flats plant is now closed, and begs the question why on Earth would anyone build a plant that dangerous downwind from a major metropolitan area? It defies human logic--we live in the antithesis of the Age of Reason.

In January of 1970, still uninformed by the government of the potential danger at the time, we purchased a home in Arvada, Colorado, a suburb north of Denver (which placed us even closer to Rocky Flats). Christopher, along with our two older children, April and Tod, moved into our new home , following his birth on January 20, 1970.

During the first couple of years, Christopher was a healthy, normal child--with no symptoms of any illnesses. Just before his second birthday, however, Christopher became desperately ill and he had to be hospitalized. He remained in the hospital For 17 days--but something was terribly wrong. Even upon his release he had trouble breathing--and this led to several invasive diagnostic tests including a lung biopsy and heart catherization.

In their puzzlement, Christopher was transferred to the University of Colorado Medical Center in Denver. Following the lung biopsy the lab tests revealed that Christopher had fibrous tissue in his lungs--not Cystic Fibrosis--but rather fibrosis from an unknown source. The medical doctors at the University of Colorado Medical Center diagnosed Christopher's illness as "Idiopathic Pulmonary Fibrosis" [fibrosis from an unknown source].

As noted, due to the government's suppression of the scientific studies which revealed the information reported, above, it was not until several years later that we learned that there may be a possible nexus between Christopher's illness and Rocky

Flats—and while this brief background defines more about Christopher's illness, and may appear to be a source of litigation, there is not enough money on earth to justify exhuming Christopher body to find out.

In 1975 the AEC was abolished as a result of Rocky Flats, resulting in creation of the U.S. Department of Energy, and currently the Energy Department.

CHAPTER FOUR

A Post Script....

ADDENDUM: To my friends in academe

Person's given to critical thinking agree that what humans most want is a "safe and sane" world in which to live, i.e., not only a safe environment in which to live and raise their children, but one that makes sense. Contemporary art such as a Clockwork Orange, and comic George Carlin seem to have best tapped into the proliferating insanity of modern life, and our growing discontent.

There are major forces afoot in the world today that are playing havoc with our social institutions: specifically, globalization and automation, and they are a major factor in pervasive unemployment in all of the OECD countries since the mid-1970's.

While these forces offer enormous social benefits, they have also created a whole new set of social problems, such as disintegration of the family, and greatly increased violence in our schools, churches and workplaces, thus calling for a whole new set of social solutions.

The underlying premise of Economic Inclusivism is that our continued application of what were once considered venerable rules, not only don't work, they are now a contributing factor in proliferating our social problems [such as the archaic notion of using "punishment" and "getting even", instead of "problem-solving" solutions to address our crime problem; and our economic solutions are based solely on "greed", i.e., the bottom line for what will most save taxes for the wealthy, not what is best for the larger society—and the "Buffett Rule" going down in flames is consummate proof]!

Lost in this, and counter-productive to a "safe and sane" world, is the common sense understanding that "altruism" and "self-preservation" are flip-sides of the same coin. Indeed, many of our current solutions could be compared to pouring gasoline on a fire to put it out.

For instance, in the 1980's, we started closing down our mental hospitals, and building prisons like there was no tomorrow. By 1990, we had passed up every other major industrial country in the world in prison inmate population (and yet our PR is that we are the most "free" country in the world?). We contributed to this by electing officials who promised to eviscerate criminals; few had the guts to step forward and tell us the truth. That this would actually make America more dangerous, not less, and it was a death knell for any politician who was honest with us.

As a result, we currently have 5% of the world's population, and 25% (one out of four) prison inmates in the world, in our prisons! To put this is in even greater perspective, if we had the same number of persons in prison, per the general population, as the rest of the civilized world we would have 400,000 in prison, not 2,400,000 as we do at present! Further, we daily turn "non-violent" offenders into "violent" career criminals, by this inept solution, when over 99% will be released back into society!

Why has the rest of the civilized world not found it necessary to use these types of extremes to address crime in their countries? China has the same incarceration rate as America, but they have a billion more people! We could send most to Harvard for what we spend on their incarceration, and every dollar we spend locking people up is a dollar that is deducted from educating our youth.

As a result of closing down our mental hospitals and asking the mentally ill to self-medicate themselves [most throw the pills away on their way out the door], all of our major cities in America are littered with homeless persons, over 60% of whom are schizophrenic, making our streets even more unsafe.

The fact is, and this will become more and more apparent the further we move into the 21st Century, that we have only one of two choices: To find work as the legal right of every citizen, or create a welfare system of some type. We have no other viable choices, and history has already shown us that welfare is more destructive, than constructive.

In time we will codify into law, in concept, the Neighbor-To-Neighbor Job Creation Act, proposed in Economic Inclusivism. Specifically, a federally mandated, mutual insurance, owned by our employed [from janitor to CEO] to provide a fund to hire/train our unemployed. It is a Pro-Market concept. Jobs beget jobs—and with a modest policy cost of 4% of salary we could reduce our unemployment rate to 3% within 6 months of passage, and as "authorized" under 15 USC § 3101. Further, this would create more "private sector" jobs in 6 months than our current "market only" path in 6 years [with the CBO projecting 7% by 2015, and 5.5% by 2017, at best][1]

HR 870, currently pending in the House also advocates the above—but is buried by the Republicans in the House, in political gridlock! Further, under the "market only" path, if the market fails—the unemployed are out of luck....

The bottom line is: The world has changed, our solutions haven't, and the result has been a disaster! It would be impossible to have over 8% unemployment [or any more than 3%], and be on the right path---and missing is a truism: That we have far more work that needs to be done, than we have persons to fill these jobs—Our inability to see this, and clouding our thinking are "sacred cows"—and a "conventional wisdom" [which was

once convinced that the world was flat]--
that still has one foot on the plantation.

Also, There are groups that want to turn
back the clock, i.e., who are anti-
globalization/modernity, but this is folly.
These forces can not be stopped, even if it
were advisable, which it is not.

How we respond to our current progress,
however, is a matter we can do something
about and Economic Inclusivism is a
comprehensive program for social-
economic/prison reforms [which have a
symbiotic relationship to each other] we
need to take so that we can effectively adapt
to these new changes.

I have titled this program, as noted:
Economic Inclusivism.

ABOUT THE AUTHOR: I was employed in our Criminal Justice System for a cumulative 20 years as a probation officer, with 5 of those years as a chief probation officer. I authored the concept of "Shock Incarceration" which became law in Kansas in 1970, and then was adopted in numerous jurisdictions in the U.S. and also spread to Europe—it is currently identified in the U.S. as "Boot Camp" [as the means to "shock" the young offender—and a total distortion of my original intent—like many ideas, once released, they take on a life of their own]. I was the Democrat candidate for Congress, District 21, TX, 2000. I would most define myself as a Social Ecologist-- [albeit my degree is in Psychology]. My web page is www.Inclusivism.org –which has been on the internet since 1996.

IN THE

Supreme Court of the United States

October Term, 1979

No. 79-1627

JAMES L. GREEN,

VS.

Petitioner,

"Excellent, excellent. A fine blend of truths, half-truths, and blatant falsehoods."

"Excellent, excellent. A fine blend of truths, half-truths, and blatant falsehoods."—in the archives of the U.S. Supreme Court, to this day....

www.ingramcontent.com/pod-product-compliance
Lightning Source LLC
Chambersburg PA
CBHW062336290526
45794CB00005B/2049